★ THE ADVENTURES OF ★
TINTIN
THE LOST TREASURE

From *The Adventures of Tintin: The Chapter Book*
written by Stephanie Peters

Based on the screenplay by Steven Moffat
and Edgar Wright & Joe Cornish

Derived from The Adventures of Tintin series by Hergé

Popcorn
ELT
Readers

Meet ...
everyone from

Tintin

This is **Tintin**. He loves to look for clues! He finds a new clue inside a model of a ship. He wants to know more!

clue

Snowy

Snowy the dog is Tintin's best friend. He loves to help Tintin.

Captain Haddock

Captain Haddock loves the sea. Tintin meets him on his ship, the *Karaboudjan*. Now Tintin has to help his new friend.

The *Unicorn*

ship

Sir Francis Haddock lived a long time ago. His ship, the **Unicorn**, went down to the bottom of the sea with all Sir Francis Haddock's treasure. After this, Sir Francis made three models of his old ship.

Ivan Sakharine

Ivan Sakharine wants to find the three models of the *Unicorn*, because he wants Sir Francis Haddock's treasure. And nothing is going to stop him!

Before you read ...
What do you think? Is Sakharine going to find the treasure?

New Words

What do these new words mean? Ask your teacher or use your dictionary.

map

She is looking at a **map**.

boat

Let's go in the **boat**.

model

He is making a **model** of a car.

box

What's in the **box**?

motorbike

This is a **motorbike**.

radio

He listens to the ship's **radio**.

rope

You need **rope** on a ship.

scroll

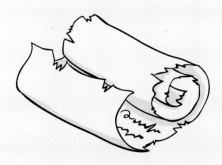

This **scroll** is very old.

seaplane

A **seaplane** can go on the water.

treasure

There's a lot of **treasure**.

'Come on!'

Come on!

Verbs

Present	Past
break	broke
take	took

☆ THE ADVENTURES OF ☆
TINTIN
THE LOST TREASURE

CHAPTER 1
The *Unicorn*

Tintin and his dog Snowy were in the town. Tintin saw a beautiful model of a ship.

'I'm going to buy that,' he thought.

He gave the money to the man and soon he had the ship in his hands.

'Its name is the *Unicorn*,' he said to Snowy.

'*The Unicorn*?' said a man behind Tintin. 'I would like to buy that model.'

'Why?' asked Tintin.

'I am Ivan Sakharine,' said the tall man. 'A long time ago Sir Francis Haddock made three models of his ship, the *Unicorn*. I have one and I want to give them all back to a Haddock now.'

But Tintin did not like Sakharine. 'Sorry, you can't buy it,' he said. He walked home with the ship.

At home, Tintin put the ship on a table.

Suddenly a cat jumped inside the room.
Snowy ran after it and ...

'Snowy!' cried Tintin. 'You broke the ship!'

Then he saw something inside it – an old scroll.
It said something about three *Unicorns* and the
light of the sun.

'I don't understand,'
thought Tintin.
'And what's this at the
bottom? I can't read it.'

Suddenly some men were outside with a big box.

'This is for you,' one man said to Tintin.

'What's in it?' asked Tintin.

'YOU are going to be in it!' said the other man.

The men put Tintin in the box and took him away.

CHAPTER 2
At sea

'Where am I?' thought Tintin. There were ropes around Tintin's hands and feet.

'You are on my ship, the *Karaboudjan*,' said a man. It was Sakharine!

'Where is the scroll from your model ship?' he asked.

'I don't know,' said Tintin.

Sakharine was angry. 'I am going to find it,' he said, 'and I am going to find the third scroll too.'

Sakharine walked out of the room. Tintin was alone in this horrible, dark place.

Or was he?

'Snowy!' said Tintin happily.

The dog was on the ship too. He helped Tintin with the ropes.

'Thanks, Snowy,' said Tintin.

He looked around the room. 'I can't use the door,' he thought. 'Where can I go?'

Then he looked outside. 'I can use the rope,' he said. Tintin started to throw the rope outside.

'Come on, Snowy,' he said. Tintin and Snowy went outside on the rope.

Soon Tintin and Snowy were in a new, dark room.

'Who are you?' said a man.

'I'm Tintin. Who are you?'

'I'm Captain Haddock. This is my ship!' the man said angrily. 'Sakharine and his men put me in here and closed the door!'

Tintin went to the door and opened it.

'Oh,' said Haddock. 'It's open!'

They started to walk through the *Karaboudjan*.

'We have to get off this ship,' Tintin said quietly. 'Do you have any ideas?'

'There's a small boat,' Haddock answered. 'We can use that.'

Tintin could hear something from behind a door.

'That's the radio room,' said Tintin. 'You and Snowy go to the boat. I want to look in here.'

Inside, Tintin found some paper next to the radio.

The Milanese singer has the third scroll in Bagghar.

'A clue! The third model ship is in the town of Bagghar,' thought Tintin. 'But who is the Milanese singer?'

He ran to find his friends.

CHAPTER 3
Boats and seaplanes

The small boat started to move away from the
Karaboudjan.

'How are we going to stop Sakharine?' asked
Tintin. 'We're in the middle of the sea!'

Suddenly he could hear something – a
seaplane. 'Sakharine's men are looking for us!'
he said.

The seaplane came down and waited on the water near their boat.

'I have to do something FAST!' thought Tintin.

He jumped into the sea and went under the water to the seaplane. He came up behind Sakarine's men and shouted, 'Put your hands up!'

The two men were frightened.

Now Tintin, Haddock and Snowy had a seaplane!

'Can you fly a seaplane?' Haddock asked.

'I think I can,' Tintin answered.

Soon they were far above the sea. This was better than the boat!

Then Captain Haddock saw the terrible rain and wind. Soon they were in the middle of it.

'I can't fly through this!' shouted Tintin.

The seaplane was not above the sea now.

'I'm taking us down!' Tintin shouted.

It was not easy, but soon they were out of the seaplane.

Tintin looked at the seaplane. 'This is never going to fly again,' he said.

They looked around. 'Where are we?' asked Haddock.

Tintin knew – they were in the Sahara Desert.

CHAPTER 4
The singer from Milan

'Bagghar is next to the sea, near the Sahara,' said Tintin. 'We have to go there and stop Sakharine.'

'How far away is Bagghar?' asked Haddock. 'The Sahara is a big place.'

'We're going to find out,' said Tintin. 'Come on!'

It was very hot, but the three friends did not stop.

'I can see Bagghar!' said Tintin. 'How are we going to find Sakharine and the third model?'

They learned the answer in the town.

'A famous singer from Milan is going to sing in Bagghar today,' said Tintin. 'She's the Milanese singer! The radio clue was about her. She works for Sakharine!'

Many people from the town waited to hear the famous singer from Milan. Tintin and Haddock waited too.

'Look,' said Tintin. 'There's the third ship in a big glass box.'

Soon the singer started to sing.

Suddenly Tintin heard something. CRASH!

'The singer can break glass,' he shouted. 'She's breaking the glass box!'

CHAPTER 5
Francis Haddock's treasure

There was glass everywhere. The people from the town started to run and shout.

Tintin saw a tall man in the middle of it all – Sakharine! He had the third model ship in his hands.

'Quick!' Tintin shouted. 'He's running for the door!'

Outside, Sakharine jumped into a car.

'Sakharine has the three scrolls now,' thought Tintin. 'How can we stop him?'

Then he saw a motorbike. 'Jump in!' he said to Snowy and Haddock.

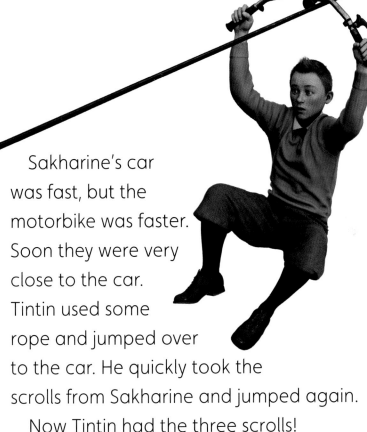

Sakharine's car was fast, but the motorbike was faster. Soon they were very close to the car. Tintin used some rope and jumped over to the car. He quickly took the scrolls from Sakharine and jumped again.

Now Tintin had the three scrolls!

With the sun behind them, Tintin could read the clue at the bottom. They were numbers.

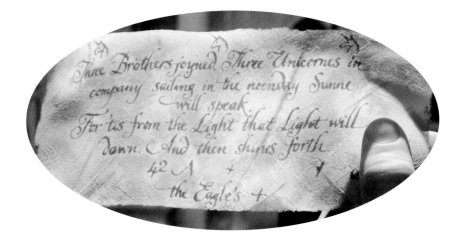

The numbers were for a place on a map.

'I know that place,' said Captain Haddock. 'It's Marlinspike Hall, the old home of the Haddocks!'

'We have to fly home,' said Tintin.

The next day the three friends went by car to Marlinspike Hall.

'I was here a long time ago,' said Haddock.

It was dark inside the house. Suddenly ...

'I can hear Snowy!' Tintin ran to find his friend.
'Look, it's another room,' said Tintin.
Inside the new room was the treasure!
'There's a scroll here, too,' said Tintin.
'It's got some new map numbers.'
The numbers were for Sir Francis
Haddock's ship, the *Unicorn*.
Tintin and Haddock smiled.
'Let's go!' they shouted.

THE SAHARA DESERT

In *The Adventures of Tintin*, Tintin, Snowy and Captain Haddock are in the Sahara Desert. Let's find out more about this very big desert.

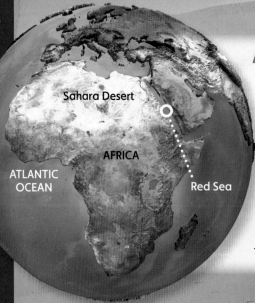

Sahara Desert

AFRICA

ATLANTIC OCEAN

Red Sea

A BIG place

The Sahara Desert in North Africa is very big – bigger than Europe! It is 4,800 kilometres from the Atlantic Ocean to the Red Sea and it is 1,600 kilometres from top to bottom.

Did you know?

Only 25% of the desert is sand. There are also mountains, rocky places and some greener places with water.

Desert animals

Life in the Sahara is hard, but some animals can live there.

Camels can live for days with no water. Their big feet help them to walk on the sand.

Camel

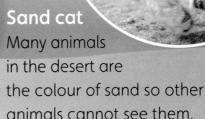

Sand cat

Many animals in the desert are the colour of sand so other animals cannot see them.

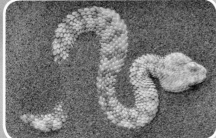

Sahara viper

This snake goes under the sand in the day. It eats at night when it is not very hot.

★
Would you like to go to the Sahara Desert? Why / why not?
★

What do these words mean? Find out.

desert   sand   mountain   rocky   snake

After you read

1 True (✓) or False (✗)? Write in the box.

a) Sakharine buys the model ship from Tintin. ☒

b) There is a scroll inside the model ship. ☐

c) Snowy helps Tintin on the *Karaboudjan*. ☐

d) Captain Haddock put the scrolls into
the model ships. ☐

e) Tintin finds a clue in the ship's radio room. ☐

f) The treasure is in Bagghar. ☐

2 Match the questions and answers.

a) Who broke Tintin's model ship?

b) Where did Tintin find the clue
about the Milanese singer?

c) Where was the third model ship?

d) In Bagghar how did Tintin
go after Sakharine?

e) Where did Tintin and Haddock
go to find the treasure?

i) In the ship's
radio room.

ii) By motorbike.

iii) It was in
Bagghar.

iv) To the old
home of the
Haddocks.

v) Snowy did.

Where's the popcorn?
Look in your book.
Can you find it?

Puzzle time!

1 Use the code and write the clue.

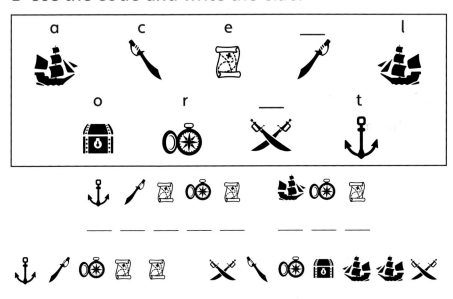

_____ _____ _____ _____

2 Do the puzzle and answer the question.

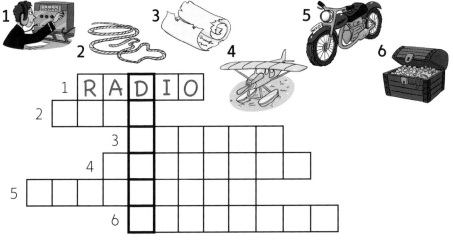

1 R A D I O

Where do the three friends fly to in the seaplane?

To the Sahara __ __ __ __ __ __

3 What is Tintin doing? Match the pictures of Tintin with the sentences.

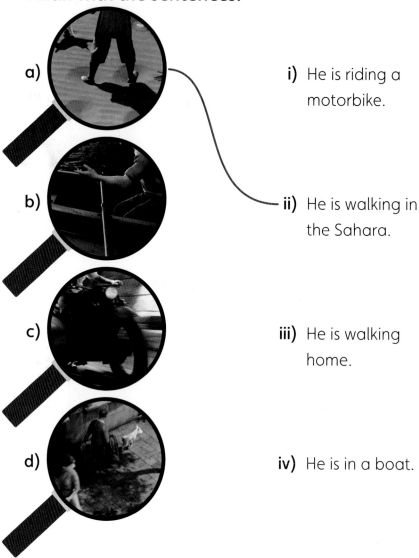

a)

b)

c)

d)

i) He is riding a motorbike.

ii) He is walking in the Sahara.

iii) He is walking home.

iv) He is in a boat.

4 Answer the questions. Then ask your friends.

a) Who is your favourite character in the story? Why?

....

b) Which is the most exciting part of the story? Why?

....

Imagine...

1 Work in pairs. Choose one of these pictures from the story.

2 Say a sentence. Your friend guesses the picture.

My name is Tintin. Who are you?

That's picture 2!

Chant

1  **Listen and read.**

Tintin's Clues

Run, Tintin, run!
What are you going to do?
There's a scroll inside the ship
And that's your first clue.

But Sakharine is here
Making problems now for you.
You want to leave the ship,
Then you find the second clue.

You're going to Bagghar.
Your friends are going too.
You must walk in the Sahara
To find the third clue.

Quick, Tintin, quick!
It's Snowy – can you hear?
He's in a new room
And the treasure is here!

2 Say the chant.